CHANGING
WITH THE TIMES

A Book of Rhymes

Andrea Steele

Changing With the Times: A Book Of Rhymes

First Edition 2025

ISBN:
Hardcover: 978-1-998245-41-3
Paperback: 978-1-998245-40-6

Cover and book design by Kabrena L. Robinson
Published by Eva-Michelle & Family Publishing
www.evamichelleandfamily.com

For my daughter, husband, and mom—your love
and support inspire me every day.

Contents

Acknowledgments   i

Introduction   ii

Mind

01	Dazed
02	Chance
04	The Season With a Reason
06	Spills of Orange
08	Before the Light Breaks
10	Pebbles
12	Imagine
14	A State of Mind

Body

16	Sparks
17	Intensity
19	Deep Desire
21	Red Romance
23	Captured
25	Obsessed
27	Dark Shades of Love
29	Drifting Apart
31	Replaced
33	Invisible Scars
35	Inhumane
37	Sinister
39	The Green-Eyed Monster
41	Soul Searchers
43	Hidden Truth
45	Trapped

Spirit

48	My Diamond
50	My Rock
52	Gone
54	Golden Memories
56	Broken
58	Another Realm

Acknowledgements

This book has been a labour of love, and I am deeply grateful to everyone who helped bring it to life.

I would like to extend my heartfelt thanks to my past student, Kabrena Robinson, for so ably assisting me in making this poetic journey a reality. The intricate layouts and illustrations are a testament to the dedication and care poured into creating a book that radiates authenticity and finesse.

To my family and friends, your unwavering support has been my anchor. Thank you for your encouragement, love, and belief in this dream.

Finally, to all the readers who will take this journey with me through these poems, may it inspire and resonate with you in unexpected ways.

With love and gratitude,

Andrea Steele

Introduction

This anthology is a deeply personal journey that was unforeseen. After experiencing profound losses, I turned to writing as a way to numb the pain and give myself space to express what I truly felt. What started as an outpouring of grief soon became something more—new ideas began to flow, and before I knew it, this collection had taken shape.

In just four unscripted days, I wrote these poems, raw and filled with the emotions I could no longer keep inside. Each one is a piece of my heart, exploring the highs and lows of being human— the warmth of love, the ache of loss, the pull of desire, and the wonder of nature.

The poems in this collection are divided into three sections: Mind, Body, Spirit. Each section reflects a different facet of our human experience, from the thoughts that keep us up at night, to the desires that drive us, to the resilience of our spirits in the face of life's challenges.

My hope is that as you read, you will find moments that resonate with your own story, whether you are seeking comfort, inspiration, or simply a quiet moment to reflect.

Thank you for joining me on this journey.

Mind

*"The mind is a garden, imagination its seeds,
and nature the endless horizon where
dreams take root and grow."*

-Proverb

Dazed

The weary sun creeps stealthily across the evening sky,
While the seagulls squawk by,
The wind caresses the battered trees,
And all the animals bow to their knees
Ready to take a long night of rest
While the birds settle in their nests.
The tall, purple-headed mountains stand proud in the distance,
Leaving nature in a trance.
Oh, how beautiful it looks–
No time for children to encounter their books.
The scene is like a finely painted canvas covering the land,
Forming a blanket of darkness with a dash of amber over the sea
and sand,
Allowing a sombre mood to linger in our hearts,
Playing with emotions that pierce our thoughts like darts.
Unmatchable, like the golden sunset;
It's just nothing like you've ever met.

Chance

For my sister Sab

So many faded dreams—
It seems
Like no one cares to fight for more.
You have so much in store
Beyond the mere trials you have encountered.
You need to be empowered;
Don't be a coward.
Stop thinking that your dreams are dead—
It's all in your head.
You need a fresh start so you can play your part.
Take a chance,
Because at a glance
I can feel your plight
Of not putting up a fight
For what you believe in.
That is a sin,
To give up so easily
When feasibly
You have all that you need
In order to succeed and lead
The best life ever,
So you should give up never.
Your desire should be a fever
That burns deep inside
For you to take a stride

To victory
And know that there is mystery
In your trajectory.
Take a plunge—
Lunge
At your dreams,
As it redeems
You to be a risk-taker,
A pace-setter.
Take a leap of faith
And lift off the weight
Of unfulfilled desire,
To decipher
Your future.
So take a chance
And dance
In your golden achievements,
And never leave your dreams to bereavements.

The Season
With a Reason

Little squirrels scurried with acorns in loads,
As dew drops fell from the pregnant clouds
Onto puny petals etched in the earth.
They smiled and stretched forth,
Like babies during birth.

Little creatures, great and small,
Knew it was going to be fall.
So they dug holes beneath the fallen leaves,
For a time later they will retrieve.

The green grass turns brown,
And everyone tries to go to town.
The sun is out,
People going all about.

The trees magically become orangey-red–
The best time of year, it is said.
While the sun, a blood-red orb,
Paints the land in a rustic hue that the leaves absorb.

Maple syrup is used this time around,
Until no more can be found.
Nature is truly spectacular–
No wonder there is a photographer,

One who captures the wondrous backdrop,
Used like a prop
In the middle of this earth, a stage
You would want to capture its essence on just a page.

Autumn! Can't wait for you to grace the land,
In another year from now, so we can all get tanned.

Spills of Orange

The golden sunset searched the horizon
For clues of a day almost done,
As a kaleidoscope of colours clashed and spun.

The fine glows of the evening into a magical scene
For lovers to hold hands and convene,
Making memories in a frame,
Never again to feel the same.

Curling their toes in the silky sand,
Listening to the brand-new band,
They take shade under the fronds of the palm,
Watching the silvery sea as it stays calm.

The soft, velvety sky
Arouses the whispers of passersby,
Enthralling the senses of those around
With the unique sound

Of birds singing melodiously, searching for their nests,
As shadows of trees casting silhouettes
Over the orange glow.
The wind caresses the waves that now gently ebb and flow.

An evening of fine dining,
With tender red petals lining
The edges of the tables,

That make even the rebels
Rethink their decisions–
Of sabotaging the beauty that lies ahead of them with precision.

A glorious backdrop on a canvas–
It's so magical it must have been captured by a painter's brush.

Before the Light Breaks

The crows squawk in the dead of night,
Searching for carrion flesh, a sweet delight.
Dark shadows crawl, encircling ghastly silhouettes,
Making the queasy hearts of mothers mourn and fret

About their children's safety
In this perilous darkness of uncertainty
Where forces of darkness squat upon a land so dead,
Waiting to steal your dreams right from your head.

This is a dread.
Strange sounds fill the harbour,
Where monsters are said to devour
The wolves that prowl,
And the owls that howl,

Creating a shrilling sound,
Making everything astound,
But it's the graveyard that seems to open up
With a pop!
Black hands rise from beneath the earth,
Trying to make you alert
To the ghostly figures that roam,
Casting a gloom
On unchartered territories.

Possibilities loom of souls to be stolen,
Before life has unfolded.
But before any foul play,
When night turns to day,

All the thoughts at night that were so perilous
In the day becomes so scandalous,
And all the fear that the darkness abbreviated
Is now alleviated.

For simply with night turning into day,
All those worries drift away,
And gory thoughts are put at bay.

Pebbles

A ripple it makes in the water,
A slight hint of how the Father
Creates magical things
With just a tiny fling.
It makes a ding
As the water quivers,
Then shivers.
Below is clear,
As it would appear—
Glass-like,
Until you strike
Straight into the middle,
Where it creates a ripple.
Little creatures swim around,
To escape the horror of a wound,
As the still water is interrupted by fine lines
With great designs.
Creating waves
That everyone craves to see—
Including me—
In the little pond
Surrounded by sand
And fertile land.
As little children lend a hand
To see who can strike straight

Into the silvery slate
That is now at peace
But will soon have a crease
Once pebbles are tossed.
So engrossed,
They stare at the place so calm,
Seeming to embalm
Its natural way.
It should stay,
But it's now so much fun
To run
Down to the pond
With pebbles in hand,
To strike straight
At the bait.
Now it bursts into ripples;
I feel like I am seeing triples
As the water scribbles
Little trickles
Across the vast expanse
Of sheer glass,
Leaving an upheaval of ultimate trespass
On this place made to enhance
This mystery of what resembles fibre-glass.

Imagine

Imagine diamonds growing on trees,
And gold was lining the breeze,
While cute little amethysts sprinkled the sea,
Reflecting sparkly stars from above,
Making us fall in love.

Tall mountains made of pure emeralds
Tower over us like heralds.
Imagine that clouds were cotton candy, all puffy and white,
Making the whole world bright
From the sight
Of light.

On the sky splattered in blue topaz,
Adding pizzazz
To the world so wondrous,
Like the flowers creating hues
Of multi-coloured shades of pink and blue.
Imagine all the grass was made of money–
Everyone would go shopping, honey!
If pebbles were pearls,
Then the swirls
In waterfalls would be made of delicate ice cream,
Laced with butter pecans, dragon stout, and pistachios
green–
Such a charming scene.

Imagine dark skies made of heavenly chocolates,
And all the cute pets
Were our best friends,
Without the furs and feathers on which you depend
For support,
With bonds of great rapport.

And imagine if all the land was filled with treasures,
Measured in everything money cannot buy,
As the world becomes a centre stage
Of beautiful things we only read on a page—
A storybook world
Where dreams are unfurled.

Imagine everything was free and woven
Into one big treat,
For everyone to share in a warm retreat.

Just imagine,
You and me,
Living happy and free.

A State of Mind

Inspired by Rosie

If I had to choose to be anything,
I would be a butterfly.

If you wonder why,
Then it's because they flit from flower to flower,
Feels like every hour—
That gives me power.
I love the smell of daffodils;
Yes, that gives me thrills.
In a world that is so free,
I like to go about and see
All the wondrous specks,
So that it reflects
On who I am as a person.
It is a lesson—
That I am but a free spirit
Who does not have a limit
On how far I will go.
So,
Leave me, let me glow
With my flow
Of
Racing across the meadows,
Chasing shadows,
Touching the new petals,
And listening to heavy metal.

I am falling deep,
As it seeps
Into
My soul,
Saying roll—
Roll down the hillside,
Without any chiding.
It's who I am inside,
So let me run wild
Like a child,
As nothing defines
Or refines
My beautiful miles.
This is my choice to be
Free,
As you can see.

Body

*"The body feels what the heart desires, and
love is the fire that warms them both."*

-Proverb

Sparks

Echoes spill across the land,
Sounding like a brand new band.
Each thrill of harmonising flow,
Tantalising down to your every toe.
The sound is so sensational,
Making folks emotional–
Beads of perspiration running down their faces,
While others have no time to tie their laces.
Waists gyrating,
Ground vibrating,
This is so invigorating.
Then it stops!
Women taking off their tops,
Soaked from sweat.
"Don't stop!" Comes as a threat.
Then the sweet sound of music fills the air again,
Instantly relieving every pain.
The mood is right,
The grip is tight,
And no one is putting up a fight.
The music creeps into the soul;
On the brain, it's taking a toll,
Creating the right energy
And formulating a synergy.

Intensity

A soothing, soft touch
I love you so much.
It makes me feel better
After receiving your letter.

With your steamy gaze,
You leave me in a daze.
Will I ever find my way through this maze
Of a love so strong?
I have waited so long
To lose this pang,
Which feels like a fang
Deep inside my troubled heart.

The sweet sensation has its start
To draw me to a depth of love
That can only be sent from above.

It's no pretence;
His love is intense.
I feel it in my bones,
The light undertones
Of a love so dangerously open
To a new horizon.

Take me to the place
Where my heart can chase
After yours in an open space,
Never to erase
A love so pure–
It's like a thousand red roses washed ashore..

Deep Desire

The night is icy fire;
I can feel his desire.
The need is dire,
My heart is a liar.

I am falling deep;
Why should I leap
Into arms so steep?
How can I sleep?

I am battling with my emotions;
Don't believe in such notions.
Why are you filling me with love potions?
I can barely keep my mind from intuitions,
Telling me to stay clear
From your stare.
You have left me bare,
But I do care.

Your touch is electric,
With eyes so magnetic.
You see that I am eclectic
And eccentric.

You leave my borders open
To new and mysterious omen.
I want to love you–

I really do,
Want you to be my beau..

This bliss,
I cannot miss;
Two hearts tangled forever.
We will part—never.

You make my heart quiver,
My butterflies shiver.
In the golden frames of my heart,
Our love will never grow apart.

Red Romance

Inspired by Ava

Red, pouting lips parted to reveal pearly white teeth.
A red dress clinging to a voluptuous body could make him whisk
her away from dinner to beneath
The sheet.
Classy red heels,
Thighs so real,
Bringing on some positive appeal.
As the wine glasses clink,
His heart begins to sink,
As she whispers sweet, sassy words in his ears–
They slice through his heart like spears.

Dangerously sexy,
She glides her heels up his leg creating a frenzy.
His body is calling;
Her language is appalling–
But he loves it anyway,
Because if night could turn to day,
The walls would speak
About the way the bed would creak.

But she stopped him right there,
On the chair,
When dinner was served.
He wished there was a room reserved.

It was her body language
That gave him an arguably safe image.
As her perfume lingered,

Oh, she felt like she was being triggered,
But she had to remind herself of the love she had waiting at home,
Choosing not to trade it for a night to roam.

She craved for new action
From this fresh attraction;
She fought her desire
For greater pleasure.
It was a one-night encounter–
He was suave, sweet, and couldn't be louder
About the passion he now felt
Beneath his belt...
The food was cold,
The story untold,
About a night of desire,
A pounding heart of fire.

The bedroom door opens,
sending chills up his spine.
Her spaghetti strap would now intertwine
With bra straps that define
That the heat was now a flame.
She was a gullible dame,
Caught in the middle of a trap.
Then she shouted, "Stop!"

His hands froze like ice
As she said, "Stop" twice.
His only thought was to devour,
But then she made him lose his power.

Captured

For my husband

His eyes gaze at my face,
Trying to erase
Every trace
Of a love story
Some find gory,
But the flame is scorching,
Torching,
Igniting my heart—
A box of fire playing its part
In making me feel stitches
That he bewitches
With his taunting gaze.
He leaves me in a daze;
How do I find my way through this maze
Of romance?
He has every chance
To take my whole heart and leave it in a trance.
My heart is a furnace,
Threaded with fine lace,
Ready for his chase.
I feel the intensity
Of this propensity,
Leaving me with such desires to enthral him
In the dim light,
Out of sight
Of human eyes—
Because inside me lies
The passion

To ease the tension
That he so poignantly expresses,
Not to other empresses—
Just to me.
Let him be
The man I see
In my dreams,
With beams
Of sudden heat
That reach my inner beat—
Of my heart
That bleeds for his touch.
Oh, I want him so much!
Fingers intertwine,
He's mine
To wine and dine;
He's so fine.
Then he kisses my lips,
And my heart does backflips—
Taking a grip
On his infused soul,
Where I want to prowl.
He radiates harmony in my mind,
Helping me to unwind.
This man is dangerously hot,
Touching the right spot.
I am weak;
He's a freak—
I cannot speak.
I am now captured by his sensitivity,
And this intensity
Will forever enthral me,
For this is where I want to be:
Soothing each other's souls
And watching how everything unfolds.

Obsessed

There is a thin line between love and hate–
It's a state
That no one should try to retaliate
But what's worse than him having a second date
With someone you hate,
Making you contemplate
Finding a new mate?

But–
I am in a rut.
I am obsessed
With the hairs on your chest
When you're not wearing a vest.

I am obsessed
With your laughter.
For me, that is torture
When I am not a part of your leisure or pleasure.

I am obsessed
With the way you look at her face,
Making me feel like there is no place
For me to retrace
Our memories that have been replaced.

I am obsessed
With thoughts of you,
Making me blue
And not staying true.

I am obsessed
With the fact that you seem happier
With the barrier
You have created around her.

I am obsessed.

Dark Shades of Love

Inspired by Nikki

He tugs at her heartstrings,
Creating a beautiful fling.
He woos her in every season,
Making her fall deeply for no real reason.
Oh, love so sweet!
Makes her heart skip a beat.
On and on they go,
Looking for the right flow–
But his heart is now an icebox,
Succinctly defiling her air sacs.
Her love is suffocating,
As his heart is no longer reciprocating.
Her heart is shattered glass,
And she thinks, "This too shall pass."
The pain pierces like shards;
It's nothing like playing cards.
The hurt is deep,
Affecting her sleep,
While he has fun,
She feels like there's nowhere to run.
She awaits sweet escape,
But feels her heart held captive by a drape.
Her heart is now a prison;
He hasn't learned his lesson.

He doesn't see the hurt he has created,
But she needs it to be alleviated.
She has recaptured her heart–
Now he's requesting a fresh start.
Her love is now restrained,
Never to be regained.
He's ready to undo his part,
But there is a padlock on her heart.
Her love has died a terrible death,
While he awaits her rekindling with bated breath.

Drifting Apart

Inspired by Oneila

I had you close–
You were a rose
In a garden filled with thorns and snakes.
I chose you, as you were different from the fakes.

Some people whisper poisonous words behind my back,
But you were my counterattack.
I depended on you,
And you on me too,

For a place to share our deepest, darkest secrets,
So there would be no regrets
About not stating how we truly feel
About our friendship and the deal.

Then,
When
We slowly drifted to separate worlds–
Oh, funny how life unfurls,
To show a sneak peek
Of how people can seek
Friendships that don't include you anymore.

My instinct tells me that that approach is poor,
For sure.
I loved her as a friend;
To her, I guess I was just a trend–

A failing spark
On which she will no longer embark.

My heart is empty,
The hurt is plenty–
A love never to be embraced,
A feeling like we will never be retraced.

A close friend
Now spends
All her time with others,
But it bothers
Me.
See,
I am still reaching out to her
On the spur
Of ten.
When she used to be my frien'.

My heart is on the floor,
Waiting for the open door
To once again hug her tightly,
But that is now just unsightly.

Replaced

You were everything I dreamt of for my prince;
That is what I tried to convince
My entire body—
That this person will embody,
My entire vision,
Of a perfect mission.

Tall and handsome,
I forgot that I was lonesome.
As I whisked him to the altar,
I thought nothing could falter.

A love so daring,
A perfect pairing,
He was so caring–

Until,

A spill
Of lies
That severed the ties
Of a love so sweet.
But deceit
Was not a part of the plan,
So I ran
Away from what seemed perfect
To dissect–

Portions that could be kept
After I wept.

It had left scars so deep,
I couldn't sleep,
And now I am an empty barrel,
Left without a quarrel,

So that my bruised heart
Could find a restart.

Even though apart
From the one I once loved,
Now I am shoved
Into a space
Where I can renew and replace
A loss so deep,
Just taking a retreat in order to keep
My heart from straying.

Lord, I will keep praying
That he will choose
To lose
Everything but my love.

But I realise now
that he won't ever again be enough.

Invisible Scars

Tears were no strangers to her eyes;
The only problem was, no one could hear her cries–
Her cries of hurt and being trapped by lies,
Lies that stood out like a sore thumb by her inner spies.

No one knew she had inner scars,
That she was living behind those invisible bars–
Bars that prevented her from aiming at the stars,
Stars that helped her inner wars.

One day he was innocent, another a monster–
Then a prankster,
If only she had a holster,
A holster with a metal frame; he would have been a spinster.
She endured the depth of words,
Words that punctured her heart like swords–
Swords that pierced through pieces of boards,
Created a soul scarred in all accords.

An escape would have been her saviour,
But that was a far-fetched favour.
He was an engraver,
Engraver of hurt that made her.

Made her feel fear and shame–
Shame that made her take the blame,
The blame of being so lame,
That she had allowed him to take all her flame.

Flames that scorched inside,
Wanting to be unleashed but had died–
Died because of the harsh reality of not taking a stride,
A stride that would have strengthened innermost pride.

The struggle was real,
Real with cries of appeal–
Appeal to stop making her feel,
Feel like a zombie, and steal her zeal.

She was a piece of sponge,
A Sponge that sucked up her emotions,
pushing her to take a plunge–
A plunge to eternity, but she had a plan to lunge,
Lunge to freedom–
Freedom that made her winsome.
God, you saved her for your kingdom.

Inhumane

Furrowed brows,
Hollowed vows,
Face strained,
Neck craned–
Never to find happiness again,

Such pain
From being estranged
By a man so uncouth;
She has lost her youth
Due to verbal scars.

He does it like a star,
With no remorse,
His voice so coarse;
He gets hoarse
From making her feel worse
About her battered heart,
Even though they are apart.

She comes up short,
To abort
The feelings she once treasured.

She was once pleasured
By a man with real feelings,
That is how she felt appealing
To him.

Now everything seems dim.
She is but a shadow of who she once was,
Tired of the fuss;
She is tired
Of being mired
In accepting the dirty words
He throws at her like swords–
Sharp as razors,
Electrifying like tasers.

She's now a tiny part of who she used to be,
Now she misses her shopping sprees.
She wants to be free,
But he makes sure that she's annoyed,
Unemployed,
So he can squeeze the light
From her bright
Personality.

Using hostility,
But she escaped the
Horrors
Of sorrows
He instilled.

Now he's being billed
For making her unskilled,
And could have been killed
By the brutality of his words
That have left her heart shattered
And battered.
As she used to cower,
And he'll never again have that power.

Sinister

Silk stockings,
Great bookings.
A black coat covers the nape of her neck;
He gives her a peck—
Checks
To see her face,
With fine black lace
Covering,
Hovering
Over any trace
Of the case.

The empty files
Unloaded in piles.
So much mystery awaits
Beyond the gates
Of her dark mansion on the hills.

All the spills
Were erased
Without a trace.
His family demands answers,
But she has sponsors
Who know how to wield power,
To lower
The tone of the scene—
So obscene.

They try to pin her
But cannot stir
An alibi.

They try,
But she's surrounded,
Grounded
By people who know how to ploy.

He was not a toy,
But money talks,
Covered by what seems like shalk.
She wears black
To prevent attack
From angry members.
She remembers
The black night;
She was in a plight,
There was a fight–
An accident, she said,
That led
To him being dead.

Now she lives with regrets
Because of threats
From a stranger.
She's in danger,
Then she's whisked off in a jet–
No more to fret
About his death.

A man she despised
Was being chastised;
Now she has revised
And devised
A plan to make her free from her history,
Free from all the treacherous mystery
Erased from her memory.

The Green-Eyed Monster

She walks into a room.
Her voice is enough for them to fall to their doom.
She wears lavish clothes;
They can't bear to see this, so they take oaths–
Oaths that they will make her pay
For looking super good every day.

She can sense their side-eyes
And questioning pries
About where her luxury is from.
"She has too many clothes," even those she wore to prom.
Their noses upturned
And the selfish envy burned
Right through their jealous hearts
Like darts.

Green with envy,
They wish she were smelly,
Like the sad things we watch on the telly. She speaks well;
Even that causes hell.
Their tone, so condescending,
Will really need some mending.

As she feels ostracised
By even those baptised,
Envy is a green-eyed monster

That no one should sponsor.
People have been killed.
Simply because they were skilled–
Skilled workers who could earn a penny
While some people don't have any.

It's not their fault
That you didn't allow yourselves to be taught,
So don't walk around with a jealous heart;
Just go out there and play your part.
The system can be very cruel,
Make sure you have enough fuel
To push through your strains
When struggles hold you down like chains–
Chains that pin you down
Until you are on the ground.
Don't be jealous of your brother;
He had to work even harder
To make it to the top.
Instead, give him a clap–
Not heavy metal sounds that go pow! POW!
Leave the green-eyed monster where it belongs
And sing our freedom songs.

Soul Searchers

They talk to your face
But stab you in the back.
You would never know anything is out of place
As everything seems to be on track.

You move mountains for them;
They make you feel at ease,
Like you're some type of rare gem–
But then they make a subtle tease.

No one sees the undercurrent
Because the tides seem normal.
No one but me seems to want to vent
Because they seem so informal.

The trick is to lure you to be comfortable;
No one is aware of the plot
Because everything seems so stable.

But others just don't see the mascot–
They feed you fine food
When you sit at their table,
That is just to allude
The disguised smirk for a smile.

Your head is now sought,
And now your 'so-called' friends
Want to hear your every thought–
But because you see the trends,
You leave them thinking
That you are just fickle;
But you are so far ahead
Ahead of the game they think you are just waiting for the 'bickle'.

Hidden Truth

You can run, but you cannot hide;
Sooner than later, you will need someone by your side.
But you are too full of pride–
Why did you even choose a bride?

So sorry for the day you took her hand;
I wish that could also be banned.
What do you think defines you? House and land?
If only her mother could still reprimand
Her.
Sir,
You need to learn how
To treat a true gem,
Instead of listening to them.
Your terrible habits you need to stem
After you have found something so rare
That everyone stops and stares.
Just be fair;
She doesn't want to be caught in a snare.

You are weak–
Why don't you turn the other cheek?
You are such a freak,
But no one would think you are such a sneak.

Who preys on innocent women
Who actually puts their trust in men,
Men like you
Who also bully–y
No one will understand it fully.
Why men like you truly
Just deserve a dolly.

This is your truth:
You are a brute
Who has taken away her youth
Just to wear a suit.
Your concrete heart
Was callous from the start.
I hope that one day she will depart,
From your jealous ass
Without a pass.

Trapped

What you see
Is just a fragment of me—
A part of who I wish to be.
So much more awaits to be set free.

In my mind, I go crazy
With thoughts that would make me seem shady.
I am but a lady,
But when I meet my alter ego, she is so dazy.

At nights, I climb poles,
Preying on weak souls.
I have ulterior motives;
Inside of me, this thought lives.

I am seen as upright,
Which makes me so uptight.
I am more than what the eyes have met,
I am just too afraid to unleash the silhouette.

Trapped within is a totally different person
Who wants to be set free for a reason.
I am just opposed to unleashing the side of me that would be
misunderstood,
But I am not living as I should.

It is so deceiving
That what you are receiving
Is just a fragment of who I am—
It's like someone sending you spam.

I crave to be revealed
But remains concealed,
Too afraid of what they might say,
Though my other self wants to stray.

Unseen dreams,
The unheard screams—
To take me on date nights,
Burning with desire to turn off the lights.

My depth
Has been kept
Buried deep inside a hallowed place
Because I don't want to be seen as a disgrace.

I don't want to live like this,
Making everything go amiss.
I want to go bungee jumping in my birthday suit;
I want to be in a hot pursuit.

But no
She won't allow
Me to escape this horrible plight
Of having to live out of sight.

Living in someone else's shadow
Is really not a choice I follow.
I want to race
Down those narrow slopes at high pace–

Giving them the adrenaline rush
That they wish for but are so hush-hush.

I want to dance on mirrored floor,
Just for you to scoop me up when you walk through the door.

I am suffocating,
Slowly relocating
My thoughts of driving a lorry–
Oh, I am too much for you, I am sorry.

I dream of being carried
Slowly off to get married,
In the sunset,
On a private jet.

In the middle of my private movie,
I want to get real groovy,
But she is so afraid
To get laid.

A masterpiece I create
With thoughts I affiliate,
But that is all it will remain,
As my hidden personality is too strong for this domain.

Spirit

"The human spirit bends with loss but rises with love.

                                    -Proverb

My Diamond

For my daughter Jenelle Steele

Fancy pinks and silvery hues–
She didn't choose;
They chose her,
Sprinkling each corner
Of her fancy bed
Where she laid her head.
It was a testimony of her girly heart;
She was so from the start.

When her eyes first met mine,
I felt like it was a sign
That she was going to be unique,
As she was born chic.

Her beautiful face
I wouldn't erase;
Holding her tiny fingers–
That memory still lingers.

A love so pure,
I knew the only cure
Would be to to love her with every ounce of my heart,
So we would never be apart.

Eyes that pierced through my barrier
Had broken down my inner warrior.
She must have seen all my heartstrings;
So much love that this little bundle brings.

A love so pure
Makes me so sure
That there would be no other such love
Except for the Father up above.

She grew into a beautiful princess,
And my love for her is no less;
As a matter of fact,
She's my whole heart
walking outside my ches'.

The centre of my world,
She's like a rare pearl
Deep inside that oyster shell.
Her words are wise, you can tell
By the many she puts under her spell.
She is and will always be My Diamond.

My Rock

For my beautiful mom, Hessie Mccarthy

Soft as a petal is her love,
A real angel sent from above.
The love she gives is not to be underestimated–
For nine long months she waited.
After she had me, she was elated;
She could hardly speak.
The love she felt she wouldn't allow my eyes to leak–
Not even for a second, as she's so meek.

If I stress,
She makes it less.
If my heart bleeds,
Her love exceeds.
If my head throbs,
She sobs.

Her heart will intertwine
With mine,
For all the love and care combine
To make sure that I am fine.

The late nights
Gave her rights
To make sure I was fed.

As a mother, she led
Me down the right path–
To take a bath,
To stay true,
And never be blue.

Her love she wrapped around my heart,
Like a blanket from the start.
Her interaction
Causes a reaction
In my brain;
She prevents me from going insane.

As I am growing up,
Faster than one gets a prenup,
She bears my pain;
I see her strain,
Her tears flow like rain.
She's my main protector
And projector;
She knows what's next
Even before I text.
She knows me inside out
And understands what I am about.
A woman of strength
Who will go to any length
To make sure that I am the best version
Without a hint of perversion.
Her navigation
Prevents me from thinking migration,
As she loves having me around;
She has found
The greatest love ever.
This love is forever;
Her heart feels mine,
And all my hurt is benign.
Her love is golden–
A mother's love,
Pure as a dove,
Is really true,
And I really love her too.

Gone

In *memory of my wonderful uncle: Altimon Powell—'Alty'*
(January 9, 1953–September 5, 2024)

Uncle Alty was a humble soul,
For his daughter, Melissa, he really played his role–
A father so devoted,
Don't know what kept him so motivated.
But his love for her was so striking,
And this was in everybody's liking.

He was so strong
And endured for long.
He smiled through his pain,
Made us cry tears like rain.

A man who loved playing domino games–
Makes us want to put his great memories in frames.
A heart so pure
Makes us miss him even more.

A man who spoke parables of wisdom;
He should inherit his Father's kingdom.
A man of his words,
Words that pierced through our souls like swords.

Though he was so sick,
We didn't know his number would have been next with a tick.
He still had so much hope;
We wondered if he was a Pope.

He showed us so much love;
Now he's flying freely like a dove.
Keep flying freely, our uncle, for if love could have saved you,
We wouldn't be feeling blue.

You will be forever etched in our hearts
Even though we are worlds apart.
Sleep on and take your rest–
You were simply the best.

Golden Memories

In loving memory of my stepdad, Leroy McCarthy ("Pops")
(February 12, 1940–July 21, 2024)

He was a true Stalwart
A man with a really big heart.
A husband, father, brother, uncle, and grandfather,
Someone who you could lean on,
who never thought it was a bother.
He was that glue that kept the family together.

I remember the many things he did that touched our lives.
I also remember the absolute joy on his face during our long
Sunday drives—
The different restaurants where we ate.
The way you would chow down the food that was set on your
plate.

All the fun times and fun places we went—
Those things will never be forgotten, as they were times well spent.

Broken

The gloom,
The doom,
Tears flow like rain,
While your heart tries to sing again.
The deafening silence torments your mind,
And your loved ones you cannot find.
It's like heaven has opened its door,
Alluding to a place more secure.
Now the emptiness
That resonates is no less
Than a thousand nails piercing through your shattered chest,
Leaving you craving more rest.
But sleep is just a memory now,
As your bed hardens like a plough.
The thoughts seem so morbid,
The fear of losing another loved one—God forbid.
The darkness squats upon the land,
Leaving you to seek comfort from someone holding your hand.
Your heart is left with jagged edges,
And your support system whispers pledges
To hold you tight
Through your terrible plight.
This ordeal
Cannot be for real.
God, you are our sovereign shield
Through this unbearable, unwanted yield—
Of not one loved one, but three.

Oh Father, we are down on one knee,
Asking for your mercy and grace
To save us from this terrible pace
Of losing loved ones without a trace.
Hearts are broken;
No words of comfort, even though spoken,
Can reach the pain that is so intense,
Not even through your closest friends.
Intestines feel knotted;
How could this trajectory have been spotted?
As no man on earth knows the hour—
Only our Saviour holds such power.
Tears flow freely like a river;
Will they stop? It feels like never.
No one sees when the stone of the tomb
Starts rolling and twisting with a boom!
Yet the spirits have been caught up yonder—
This becomes the greatest wonder.
Oh death! When will you lose your sting?
To the hearts of many, sadness you always bring.
So leave;
Let us grieve,
For only God knows how to relieve
The stress,
The mess,
Of our broken dreams.
But He will be our only comfort,
It seems.

Another Realm

In Loving Memory of My Father, DestyVal Clarke (DADA)

Don't search for me;
I am somewhere across the sea.
I have had golden years,
So hold back your tears.

Don't cry for me;
I have had time to self-reflect and sip my tea,
Plenty of fun
Under the sun.

Don't wait for me;
I am falling deeply, you see,
Beneath the yellow sunset–
So please don't fret.

Don't sigh for me;
I am with thee,
Roaming the land,
Offering a helping hand.

Don't come with me;
My friends I see
Every day when we meet
Under the billows so sweet.

Dream of me,
For I am happy,
Free as a bee;
I have my Father's key.

As my soul soars across the shores,
I pray my soul to save
As I am no longer in the grave.

Freedom I feel as I drink milk and honey;
In this place of pearly gates, it is always sunny.

Sing for me,
Set me free,
But remember I am always with thee.

www.ingramcontent.com/pod-product-compliance
Lightning Source LLC
Chambersburg PA
CBRC090824120626
46547CB00007B/602